SET PLAYS TO SCORE

Bob Huggins

COACHES CHOICE™

ISBN: 1-58518-176-5

Library of Congress Catalog Card Number: 99-69028
Cover Design: Charles L. Peters
Interior Design: Janet Wahlfeldt
Cover Photos: Brian Spurlock
Editor: David Hamburg

Coaches Choice Books is a division of: Coaches Choice
                                           P.O. Box 1828
                                           Monterey, CA 93942
                                           Web Site: http://www.coacheschoiceweb.com

CONTENTS

Basketball offenses are usually categorized as either terminal action (set plays), continuity, or freelance. Each has individual strengths and weaknesses. Continuity offenses (such as flex) allow your players to continue to run a pattern without having to stop and reset, but also allow the defense to anticipate the next move. Freelance offenses give players with great individual skills a chance to play without many restrictions, but some coaches do not provide enough control when attempting to get players to play within more specific offensive roles. Set-play offenses allow a coach to have more control over how and where shots are taken. They also help him to make sure that the shot clock is not a factor.

In this book, I am going to give you a variety of set plays that will allow you to use the individual talents of specific players and still maintain a team concept within your offense. These sets will provide opportunities to isolate any positions on the floor. The goal of any offense is to get easy baskets. Set offensive patterns should complement your fast-break pattern and can be used as a change-up from or entry into continuity or freelance offenses. When your fast-break attempt is stopped, your team should have a good set attack to rely on.

Set offenses should be based on sound offensive fundamentals of spacing, screening, offensive rebounding and defensive balance and employ aggressive pressure and movement. It is essential that you follow the philosophy of identifying the strengths of your team and focusing on a few sets that fit their skills. Doing a few things well is much better than doing many things adequately. You should be as knowledgeable as possible about different kinds of sets and then choose a few sets that meet your needs and are appropriate to the age and ability of your athletes. Having a minimum number of plays and options will allow the players to know and execute the offensive plan. Repetition of drills designed to teach the fundamentals of the sets will train them thoroughly in the details necessary to successfully defeat defenses during crunch time. Time needs to be spent working on plays to each side of the floor and with different combinations of players.

One of the things an offensive coach who uses set patterns must be careful of is not to make his players "machine-like" in their movement and decision making. They must not lose their ability to "react and play" when the defense breaks down. Too many options may confuse your team and too few options for your level may allow a good defensive team to stymie your attack.

I hope that this book will provide you with some choices that fit your personnel. Ideally, some of these sets will allow you to do the following:

- Play to your team's strengths

- Exploit the weaknesses of your opponents

- Create desired matchups

- Isolate poor defenders to score or create foul opportunities

- Allow your team to have more defined roles

- Keep the ball in the hands of your better ball handlers and decision makers

- Place your players where they can be the most effective

- Rely on execution to defeat good defenses

- Be compatible with your fast-break system, as well as other offensive schemes

- Provide for offensive rebounding

Over the years, these plays have proven very effective for us in trying to get the most out of our personnel. Every year, we must evaluate our team and decide on which sets are the best fit. We will naturally rely more heavily on these plays for our better offensive players, depending on what they can or cannot do each ensuing year.

Hopefully, they will prove to be as beneficial to you and your team as they have been to us. Have a great season and win them all.

COACH = **C**

OFFENSIVE PLAYER = ○

SPECIFIC OFFENSIVE PLAYERS = ① ② ③ ④ ⑤

OFFENSIVE PLAYER WITH THE BALL = ♂

DEFENSIVE PLAYER = X

SPECIFIC DEFENSIVE PLAYERS = X_1 X_2 X_3 X_4 X_5

PASS = - - - →

CUT OR PATH OF THE PLAYER = ———→

DRIBBLER = ∿∿∿

SCREEN = ———┤

OFFENSIVE PLAYER O4 WHO STARTS WITH THE BALL, PASSES IT TO O2 AND THEN SCREENS FOR O3, WHO USES HIS SCREEN TO CUT

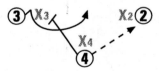

CHAPTER 1

Plays from a High Post Set (2-1-2 or 2-3)

OVERVIEW OF HIGH POST SET

The high post set usually is run from either a 2-1-2 or 2-3 alignment. It is probably one of the oldest, but still one of the most commonly used, of all present-day offensive attacks. In this system, one player is placed near the middle of the foul line, in order to provide spacing and use his individual talents. In any offense, one of the most difficult places on the floor to defend is the high post. All the other offensive players are within one pass; the high post area is usually within the shooting range of most players, and there is room to penetrate if the defense overplays the shot.

Ideally, a high post player can shoot, pass and penetrate. Even though most high post players are usually your taller players, many times a smaller, quicker, more active player may be the best choice for this position. A post player stationed at the foul line with room to operate is more difficult to defend for a larger, slower defender than one who is located in the low post with limited space to move. When a taller, slower player is guarding an active offensive player at the high post, the slower player has difficulty reacting, and his lack of quickness is magnified further from the basket. Taking a taller defender away from the basket can neutralize the advantage he has in rebounding. Also, an active player coming from the high post can be difficult to block out and be a very effective offensive rebounder. When the player you select to play the high post has a combination of size and agility, he will add many additional dimensions and versatility to this offensive set. Most of the set plays we run from this alignment revolve around the high post man.

The four perimeter players must be able to shoot, drive, set and use screens and cut without the ball. Because the low post area is vacant, you will often see occasions in these set plays when we move one of the four perimeter players into the low post in an effort to isolate him with passing angles from the corner, wing or high post. The spacing provided by this set makes it difficult for the defense to trap, double-team or even overplay the wings without opening up easy, open cuts for the perimeter players.

The cutting and screening possibilities provided for the perimeter players by having a man in the high post cause many defensive adjustments and allow a coach to identify and isolate advantageous matchups or weak individual defenders. The more movement your sets can provide for their perimeter players, the more lanes open up for passing, driving and cutting.

The plays diagrammed and described in this chapter are all out of the 2-1-2 or 2-3 set. Some of the sets are entry plays into a continuity offense, while others are terminal-action plays in which the offense must reset if the first attempt did not provide scoring opportunities. Some of the plays "build" from one to the next. We have attempted to give you examples of plays that use cutting, single screens, double screens, staggered screens and individual isolations for each player. The diagrams usually show the set being run on one side of the floor, but nearly all the plays can be run to either side with identical results.

Regardless of the type of alignment you choose for your team, it will not operate properly unless the individual skills and techniques of your players are mastered. Stress the small details and the quickness of execution. Be prepared for defensive adjustments your opponents may make against this set. For example, if your team is not ready to counter a defensive team that overplays the entry pass to the wing, or switches screens, these plays will not be effective. But if your team is prepared to counter defensive pressure, the basic sets will even be more effective.

ONE CUTTER FOR A LAY-IN

Diagram 1

O1
- Enters the ball to O3 on the wing

- Makes a hard basket cut, using the back screen set by O5

O2
- Stays spaced 12–15 feet from O1 and a step behind the line of the ball

- When the ball is entered to O3, O2 spaces away from O5 12–15 feet

O3

- Makes an "L" cut from the block up the lane to the wing

- Catches and squares up to the basket, looking for O1 rubbing off O5

- Reads O5's defender to see if he is hedging off to help on the cut; if not, then O1 should be open early to receive the ball

O4

- Positions himself on the opposite block, preparing to duck in big for the basketball

O5

- Starts in the middle of the foul line

- Steps to the side elbow and sets a back screen for O1

- If O5 has a tendency to exaggerate his position on the screen and is getting called for fouls, he can turn and face the basket and set the screen with his back

ONE CUTTER FOR A POST-UP – CONTINUATION OF PREVIOUS PLAY

Diagram 2

O1

- Has made the basket cut and was not open

- As the ball is passed to O5, he sets up his man by taking him into the key, preparing for the down screen by O3

- Comes off the down screen ready to shoot or feed the ball inside to O3, who has posted up strong after screening

02

- Maintains spacing away from 05, moving without the ball to ensure a good passing angle as he looks to receive a pass from 05 so he can feed 04 in the post

03

- Has the ball on the wing after 01 has cut and wasn't open

- Passes to 05 as he steps out off the back screen

- Then sets a solid down screen for 01

- After screening, he posts up strong, looking for the post feed from either 05 or 01

04

- As soon as 05 receives the ball from 03, 04 steps big into the lane, looking for a high-low pass from 05

05

- Steps up and to the ball after setting a screen for 01; it is important that he catches the ball within the foul circle so his next pass is not too long

- First look is for 04 posting if he has his man behind him; second look is to 01 coming off the down screen; third look is to 03 posting up after screening for 01

HIGH-LOW FEED WHEN 04 IS FRONTED—CONTINUATION OF PREVIOUS PLAY

Diagram 3

01

- Same as previous play

O2
- Moves without the ball to maintain spacing and create an angle for O5 to pass the ball to him out of the high post

- As he moves and relocates, he reads how X4 is defending O4

- If X4 is below O4, he anticipates that O5 will feed him the ball from the high post

- If X4 has denied the pass from O5 by being on top of O4, O2 should have a great passing angle as O4 pins and holds X4 on his top side

O3
- Same as previous play

O4
- Attempts to step over and pin X4 below him so he can receive the high-low pass from O5

- But if X4 denies the cut by being on top of him, then he pins X4 on his high side and anticipates his post feed from O2 on the wing

O5
- As he catches the ball from O3, he reads how O4 is being defended

- If X4 is on the high side, he looks to kick the ball out to O2 for the post feed to O4

ONE CUTTER FOR DRIBBLE WEAVE—OPTION FROM SAME SET

Diagram 4

O1
- After O1 has come off the down screen, he sets his man up and takes a handoff from O5, looking to attack the basket with the dribble

- On the dribble penetration, he attempts to draw X4 to come help so he can drop the ball off to O4

- He can continue the weave by handing off to O2 and rolling to the basket, looking for a return pass

O2
- Maintains spacing while O1 takes the handoff from O5

- As O1 begins to penetrate, he spots up on the three-point line for a kick-out pass

- If O1 dribbles at him, he continues the weave by taking the handoff, looking to attack the basket, or handing off to O3 and rolling to the basket

O3
- Reads to weave with O1 and O5 and clears to the corner

- Spots up, looking for a kick-out if his man sags to help

- Continues the weave by taking the handoff from O2

O4
- Steps out of the lane after posting up and readies himself for the drop-off pass if X4 helps on penetration

- Steps out to the corner if the weave continues with O2

O5
- Takes the ball toward O1 with a hard dribble or two; sets a screen on X1 as he hands off to O1; and then rolls to the basket, looking for a return pass

ONE CUTTER TO CROSS SCREEN

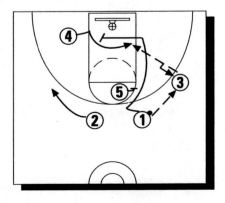

Diagram 5

O1

- Enters the ball to O3 on the wing and makes the hard basket cut off O5's back screen

- Gets to the block and goes across the key to screen for O4

- This provides an opportunity for a guard to screen a post player; if a team switches cross screens, the O4 should have a mismatch

O2

- Maintains spacing from O1 until he passes and cuts, and then spaces from O5

- Spots up on the three-point line and calls for the ball if his man sags to help

O3

- L-cuts to get open on the wing

- Catches the ball and squares to the basket, looking for O1 making a basket cut off O5's screen, and then O4 coming across the key from O1's screen

O4

- Sets his man up by taking him higher or lower and then cuts off the opposite direction to the ball

- Posts hard and calls for the ball

O5

- Steps to the elbow to set the back screen and steps back out with timing

ONE CUTTER TO CROSS SCREEN—DOWN SCREEN—CONTINUATION OF PREVIOUS PLAY

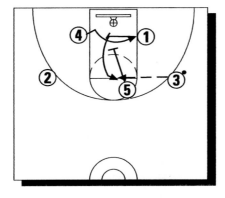

Diagram 6

01

- After he has set the cross screen for 04, he receives a down screen from 05

- He comes off the down screen in the middle of the key, looking for the jumper or high-low pass to 05

02

- Maintains spacing from 01 and then 05

- Spots up on the three-point line and calls for the ball if his man sags to help

- Can receive a kick-out pass from 01 to feed 05 at the post after his down screen

03

- Receives the ball on the wing and reads the cross screen

- If 04 is not open on the cross screen, he looks for 01 coming off 05's down screen

04

- Comes off the cross screen and posts up hard on the block

05

- As 01 starts the cross screen, he goes into the middle of the key, looking for 01's defender and sets a down screen on him

- After screening, he posts and looks for the ball from either 01 or 02

- If the defense switches the down screen, he should have a mismatch at the post, and 01 should have a mismatch on the perimeter

ONE CUTTER INTO FLEX PATTERN

Diagram 7

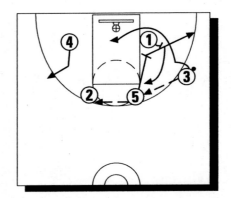

Diagram 8

01

- Enters the ball to 03 and makes a hard basket cut off 05's screen

- After 03 reverses the ball to 05, he sets a baseline back screen for 03

- After screening, he receives a down screen from 05 and goes up to the elbow, looking for a jumper

02

- Maintains his 15–17-foot spacing and, after receiving a pass from 05, first looks for 03 coming off the baseline screen

- Second look is to 01 coming off the down screen set by 05

- Third look is to swing the ball to 04 on the wing

03

- After catching the ball on the wing, he looks for 01 on the basket cut

- Then reverses the ball to 05 stepping out off the screen at the elbow

- After passing to 05, he sets his man up and comes off the baseline back screen set by 01, cutting hard to the opposite block, looking for the pass

04

- As the ball is being swung to 02, he makes an L cut to get open on the wing

- If he receives the ball from 02, his first look is to 03 cutting off the baseline screen

05

- Sets the back screen for 01 to initiate the first cut

- Steps up off the back screen and receives the pass from 03 and looks to immediately swing the ball to 02

- After passing to 02, he sets a down screen for 01 to get open at the elbow and then pops to the corner

Flex is a continuity offense that utilizes the principle of screening the screener.

HIGH POST DOWN

Diagram 9

Diagram 10

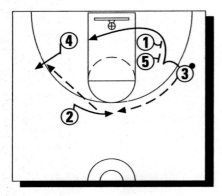

Diagram 11

Diagram 12

O1

- Enters the ball to O3 on the wing and makes a hard basket cut off O5's screen

- Stays in the low post as the ball is being reversed, setting a double screen with O5 (Diagram 9)

- O3 uses the screen by setting up his defender and going either high or low off the double (Diagram 10)

- After O3 has passed his line of vision, O1 comes off a staggered screen set first by O5 and then by O2; he looks to receive the ball for a shot near the top of the key (Diagram 11)

- If his shot is not there, he reverses the ball to O2, and the play can continue with O4 coming off the double set by O3 and O5 (Diagram 12)

O2

- Sets his man up and goes toward the ball for a reversal pass from O3 (Diagram 10)

- Plays out of the middle of the floor so there is a good angle to feed either O3 coming off the double, or reverses the ball to O4 (Diagram 10)

- After reversing the ball, he goes into the key and finds O1's defender to set the second part of the staggered screen (Diagram 11)

- After setting the screen, he flares out to the wing for a potential pass from O1, where he would look for O4 coming toward him off the double (Diagram 11)

- If the play were to continue, he would be the man coming off the double screen after reversing the ball

O3

- Makes an L cut to get open on the wing, catches the ball and looks for O1 on a basket cut (Diagram 9)

- Reverses the ball to O2 and goes off the double screen set by O1 and O5 (Diagram 10)

- Looks to receive the ball from either O2 or O4

- If he doesn't get the pass, he becomes the bottom man in the double screen with O5 (Diagram 11)

- If the play continues, and after O4 uses the double screen, O3 would come off a staggered screen to the top of the key, and the pattern continues (Diagram 12)

O4

- Starts on the opposite block and breaks to the wing when O2 receives the reversal pass (Diagram 10)

- Catches the reversal pass and looks for O3 coming off the double

- If O3 is not open, he reverses the ball to O1 at the top of the circle and cuts off the double screen (Diagram 12)

- If he does not receive the ball, he becomes the bottom man in the next double screen set

O5

- Starts in the middle of the foul line and steps to the elbow to set the initial screen for O1 to basket cut (Diagram 9)

- He follows O1 to the low post and becomes the top man on a double screen for O3 (Diagrams 9 and 10)

- As O3 passes the screen, he sets a screen for O1

- After screening for O1, he continues across the lane to join O3 as the top man in the double screen for O4 (Diagrams 11 and 12)

- He continues the same pattern for as long as the offense continues

CUTTER—OFF GUARD ISOLATION

Diagram 13   **Diagram 14**

This play is run to isolate a guard in the post area.

O1

- Enters the ball to O3 on the wing and spaces away for a potential reversal pass

- It is important that he stays spaced away from O5 so his man cannot sag and help on O5 while he is trying to make a high-low feed to O2

O2

- As the ball is entered to O3, O2 takes a hard cut to the block off O5's screen

- He goes in a straight line right for the block, looking for the ball as he cuts

- If he is not open on the cut, he posts and calls for the ball from O3

- If O2 is fronted, he pins and seals his defender and O3 reverses the ball to O5 for the high-low pass

O3
- L-cuts to receive the ball on the wing and immediately looks for O2 cutting

- If O2 is not open on the cut, he lets him settle in the post and feeds him the ball

- If O2 is being fronted in the post, he passes to O5, who can high-low feed to O2

O4
- Begins the play on the opposite block, and as O3 catches the entry pass, he pops out to the wing to draw his defender away from the post

- He maintains spacing, preparing to catch and shoot or feed to O2

O5
- Starts in the middle of the foul line and back screens for O2 on the entry pass

- After screening, he steps to the ball and reads how O2 is being defended

- If O2 is being fronted, he flashes toward O3 and receives the ball for a high-low feed to O2

BALL-SIDE GUARD LOB

Diagram 15

O1
- Enters the ball to O3 on the wing and starts to follow the pass toward O3

- Changes his direction and cuts hard off O5's screen, looking for the lob

- He should start looking for the ball as soon as he clears the screen at the high post

O2
- Occupies his defender by coming toward O3 as if he were looking for a reversal pass

O3
- L-cuts to get open on the wing

- Catches the ball and looks first to O4 in the block, second to O1 going to the basket for the lob and third for O5, who has a great angle to feed the ball to O1 in the post

O4
- Starts on the block away from the ball

- Cuts hard to ball-side low post and calls for the ball; this move drags his defender away from the area we are trying to lob to

O5
- Begins in the middle of the foul line

- Steps to the ball-side elbow and sets a back screen for O1, who is going for the lob

- After screening, he steps back to the ball inside the key area and looks to receive the ball and feed high-low to either O4 or O1, both of whom are in the key, sealing their defenders off

BALL-SIDE LOB TO POST ISOLATION

Diagram 16

Diagram 17

O1

- Enters the ball to O3 on the wing, starts to follow his pass, and then cuts hard off O5, looking for the lob

- If the lob is not there, he goes weakside block, looking for a post feed from either O5 or O2

O2

- Stays spaced 15–17 feet from O5

- Receives the reversal pass from O5 and looks to feed O1 on the block

O3

- L-cuts to catch the ball on the wing

- Catches and squares, looking to pass first to O4 in the post, second to O1 on the lob and third to O5 for the high-low feed

O4

- Starts on the block away from the ball and cuts hard to the ball-side low post and calls for the ball

O5

- Begins in the middle of the foul line and sets a back screen for O1 going for the lob

- Steps back to the ball inside the circle and, after catching the reversal pass, looks to feed O1 or O4 at the low post or swing the ball to O2, who attempts to do the same

BALL-SIDE GUARD LOB TO A DOUBLE SCREEN

Diagram 18

Diagram 19

This play is a continuation of the ball-side guard lob play and begins where the players are at the end of that play.

O1
- Has made the cut off O5, looking for the lob, and is in the weakside block, looking for the high-low feed

- He quickly reverses direction and comes off the double set by O3 and O4, looking for the jumper

O2
- Stays spaced from O5 and could be used to feed O1 in the weakside post

O3
- After his L-cut to receive the entry pass and the reads he makes on the lob play, he reverses the ball back to O5 and sets a double screen with O3 to be used by O1

O4
- After cutting to the ball-side post, as O5 receives the pass at the high post, he turns back to the key and sets a double screen with O3

- He can basket cut if his defender overplays the double screen

O5
- After setting the back screen for O1 on the lob, he steps back toward the ball (staying inside the circle) and receives the pass from O3 and looks for O1 coming off the double

BALL-SIDE GUARD LOB TO A DOUBLE SCREEN—CONTINUATION

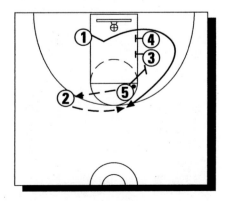

Diagram 20

O1

- As O1 comes off the double screen set by O3 and O4, he looks for the pass from O5

- If O5 swings the ball to O2, he knows that he is going to receive a screen from O5 and sets his man up to get open at the top of the circle

- O1's defender has had to fight through a back screen, immediately to a double screen and then into a third screen by O5

O2

- He stays spaced from O5, and if O1 is not open coming off the double, he gets a pass from O5 and looks for O1 coming off a screen toward the top of the circle

O3

- Same as the previous play

- Always looks to slip to the basket if his defender cheats out on the double

O4

- Same as the previous play

O5

- Same as the previous play, except that if O1 is not open coming off the double, then he swings the ball to O2 and screens down for O1 to get open at the top of the circle

FORWARD ISOLATION

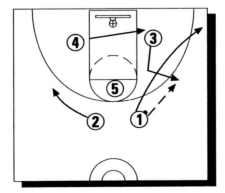

Diagram 21

01

- Enters the ball to 03 on the wing

- Runs a *shallow cut* hard to the corner

- Sets up to receive a pass for either a jumper or a post feed to 04

02

- Maintains his spacing from 05 to occupy his defender or get a kick-out for a shot

03

- L-cuts to get open on the wing

- Catches and squares up to make the following reads

- Passes to 04 in the post

- Passes to 05 for the high-low if 04 is being fronted or his defender gets caught on the low side

- Pass to the corner to 01 if 04's defender gets caught on the high side

04

- As soon as 03 catches the ball on the wing, he flashes hard to the ball-side low post and works to receive the ball

- He reads how his defender is playing him and then pins him on whichever side he is on and anticipates where the entry pass will come from

- If the defender is behind, he should get the pass from 03

- If the defender is in front or on the low side, the pass should come from 05

- If the defender is on the high side, he will get the pass from 01 in the corner

05

- Makes himself available in the high post, reads how 04's defender is playing him and either looks for an open shot or a high-low feed to 04

CENTER ISOLATION

Diagram 22

O1

• Enters the ball to O3 on the wing and shallow cuts to the corner

• Prepares to get open for a shot or a post fed to O5 if X5 is caught on the high side

O2

• Maintains spacing to occupy his man or get open for a shot if his man sags off

O3

• L-cuts to receive the ball on the wing and makes the following reads:

—Passes to O5 in the low post if his defender is behind him

—Passes to O4 in the high post if X5 is fronting or caught on the low side

—Passes to O1 in the corner if X5 gets caught on the high side in the post

O4

• Starts low post opposite and cuts hard into the high post area

• Looks to catch the ball for either a shot or a high-low feed if X5 is fronting, or on the low side when defending the post

O5

• Starts in the middle of the foul line and cuts hard to the low post as O3 receives the ball on the wing and O1 has crossed in front of O3 on his shallow cut to the corner

- Posts hard, pinning and sealing his defender on whichever side he is playing him

- If the defender is behind, he should receive the pass directly from 03

- If the defender is in front or on the low side, he should anticipate the pass coming form 04

- If the defender is on the high side, he expects the pass to come from 01 in the corner

SHUFFLE CUT THE FORWARD

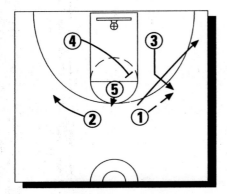

Diagram 23

Diagram 24

01
- Enters the ball to 03 on the wing and shallow cuts to the corner

02
- Maintains spacing from 05

- Prepares to catch the ball on a reversal and feeds 03 cutting to the basket off 04's *shuffle screen*

- If 03 is not open, he can hit 04 rolling back to the ball

03
- L-cuts to get open on the wing

- Catches, squares up and reverses the ball back to 05

- After passing, he cuts *shoulder to shoulder* off 04's shuffle screen to the basket for a lay-in

- If 03 does not receive the ball on the shuffle cut, he clears to the corner to open up the lane area

04
- Starts low on the opposite block and, as 03 receives the entry pass, crosses the lane and sets a solid shuffle screen for 03 after he has passed the ball

- After 03 has cleared his vision off the screen, he rolls back to the ball

- If he dose not receive the ball and wants the play to continue, he sets another shuffle screen, this time for 02

05
- Starts in the middle of the foul line and pops out to the top of the circle to reverse the ball to 02

SINGLE OR DOUBLE FOR YOUR BEST SHOOTER
Note: This play can be run for either guard.

Diagram 25   **Diagram 26**

01
- Enters the ball to 03 on the wing and makes a hard basket cut off 05's back screen

- Sets his man up by stepping into the key and reads his defender

- He can come off a double screen set by 03 and 05

- If the defense overplays toward the double screen, he can use the single screen set by 04 on the other side

O2

- Maintains spacing and breaks back to the ball to receive a pass from O3

- Looks to pass the ball to O1 coming off either the double or single screen

- Also needs to be ready to pass to any screener whose man overplays and allows a basket cut

O3

- L-cuts to get open on the wing

- Receives the pass and squares to the basket, looking for O1 on a basket cut

- Reverses the ball to O2 and sets a double screen with O5 for O1

- Can slip the screen if his defender overplays

O4

- Starts on the block opposite the ball and sets the single screen for O1

- Can slip the screen on an overplay by his defender

O5

- Starts on the middle of the foul line and goes down with O3 to set the double screen after O3 has reversed the ball to O2

ON-THE-BALL SCREEN FOR A POST ISOLATION—WEAK SIDE

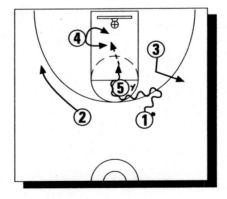

Diagram 27

O1

- Dribbles the ball toward the sideline to get a better angle

- Reverses his dribble and drives hard off O5's ball screen, trying to turn the corner to the basket

- This should freeze O4's defender in a help situation, enabling O4 to step in and seal

- Tries to draw X4 to him and then deliver the ball to O4 in the post

O2
- Slides over to the offside wing, preparing to catch and shoot or feed to O4

- O2 should receive the ball if O4 has pinned his defender on his high side

O3
- L-cuts out to the wing, acting as a decoy and occupying his defender

O4
- Starts on the weakside block

- Waits until O1 comes off the ball screen and then reads X4 and moves to an open area in the post or ducks in hard and pins his defender

O5
- Waits for O1 to change direction with his dribble and then steps in and sets a ball screen

- After screening, he steps back to get ready for a reversal pass from O1 and looks for his shot

ON-THE-BALL SCREEN FOR A POST ISOLATION—STRONG SIDE

Diagram 28

Diagram 29

01

- Dribbles the ball towards the sideline to improve his angle to the screener

- Reverses his dribble and comes hard off O5's ball screen, attempting to turn the corner to the basket

- If he can turn the corner, he takes it as deep as he can go and looks to score

- If he can't turn the corner, he reverses the ball back to O5 at the opposite elbow

02

- Slides over to the offside wing to spot up and catch a kick-out pass and score if his man helps on the driver

03

- L-cuts out to the wing to occupy his defender and keep him away from the basket

04

- Starts on the weakside block and cuts to the ball side *before* O1 comes off the screen

- Prepares to catch a pass from O1 after penetration

- Then ducks in hard if O1 has to reverse the ball to O5

05

- Sets a ball screen for O1 as he reverses his dribble

- Then steps back, looking for a reversal pass from O1 if he can't turn the corner to the basket

- If he receives the pass, he can either shoot or post feed to O4, who has ducked into the post

PRESSURE RELEASE FOR A LAY-IN

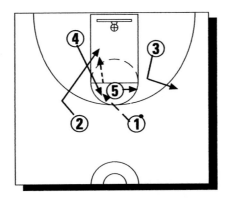

Diagram 30

01

• Enters the ball to O4, who has flashed to the opposite elbow

02

• Is overplayed by his defender to prevent a reversal pass, so he plants and makes a quick change-of-direction cut to the basket as soon as the ball is passed to O4

03

• Makes an L-cut from the ball-side block to the wing, occupying his man and keeping him out of the key area

04

• Starts on the weakside block and flashes to the opposite elbow, looking for a pass from O1

• He receives the pass from O1 and immediately looks for O2 back cutting to the basket

05

• Starts in the middle of the foul line

• Moves over to the ball-side elbow, opening up the opposite elbow area for O4 to cut

PRESSURE RELEASE FOR A DOUBLE SCREEN

Diagram 31

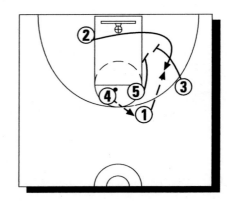

Diagram 32

This play can be used as a continuation of the previously described play (Pressure Release for a Lay-in (Diagram 30)

O1

- Enters the ball to O4, who has flashed to the opposite elbow

- Stays spaced 15–17 feet away from O4 so his defender cannot sag and help and so he can get open for a return pass

- He moves to get himself open and receives the reversal pass from O4

- His first look is to O2 coming off the double screen set by O3 and O5

- Reads how the defenders in the double screen are playing O2's cut, and if either of them cheats out to cover O2, he looks for O3 or O5 slipping the screen and going to the basket

O2

- In diagram 31, O2 is being overplayed by X2 and is unable to receive a direct pass from O1

- As O4 flashes up to the elbow, he sets his man up and takes a quick change-of-direction cut to the basket so that as soon as O4 has caught the ball, he is open to receive the ball

- He holds at the post while looking for a pass from O4

- As soon as O4 reverses the ball to O1, he cuts hard across the key and off the double screen set by O3 and O5

03
- Starts at the ball-side low post and L-cuts up the lane to get open on the wing, just as he has done in all the plays described in the previous pages

- Occupies his man away from the basket and out of the key area so it is open for 02's basket cut

- As the ball gets reversed back to 01, he moves back down toward the key to set a double screen with 05

- Reads his defender to see if he overplays the cutter, and if he does, 03 should slip the screen and go to the basket for a pass from 01

04
- Starts on the weakside block

- Flashes to the opposite elbow to receive the pass from 01

- He quickly pivots and looks for 02 making a back cut to the basket, behind him

- If 02 is not open on the back cut, he allows him to establish position in the low post and looks to feed him the ball

- If nothing is open on either the back cut or in the post for 02, he reverses the ball to 01 so the ball can be passed to 02 coming off the double screen

05
- Starts in the middle of the foul line

- Moves to the ball-side elbow to open up a passing lane from 01 to 04 on the opposite elbow

- As the ball is being reversed from 04 to 01, he moves down the lane and sets a double screen with 03

- While setting the screen, he reads how the defense is playing the cutter, and if his defender cheats out to help on 02, he slips the screen and cuts to the basket and looks for a pass from 01

PRESSURE RELEASE FOR AN ISOLATION

Diagram 33

Diagram 34

O1

- Enters the ball to O4 as he flashes up to the opposite elbow

- Stays spaced away from O4 for a potential return pass

O2

- He is being overplayed by X2 so that he cannot receive a direct pass from O1

- Makes a hard back cut to the basket as soon as O4 receives the ball from O1

- Instead of holding at the post, he clears immediately toward the double screen set by O3 and O5, creating a clear-out isolation for O4

O3

- L-cuts to get open on the wing

- Occupies his man away from the basket

- Sets a double screen with O5 further off the lane than the previous play so that the key area remains more open

O4

- Starts on the weakside block and flashes up to the opposite elbow to receive a pass from O1

- Looks for O2 back cutting to the basket behind him

- Squares up, and as soon as O2 clears the lane, he takes his man one-on-one to the basket

O5

- Starts in the middle of the foul line and moves to the elbow to open up space for O4

- Sets a double off the lane with O3

PITCH-BACK TO CLEAR OUT

Diagram 35

Diagram 36

O1

- Enters the ball to O4 on the wing and follows his pass for a pitch-back from O4

- After O4 clears to the opposite side of the key, O1 passes the ball to O3 at the ball-side elbow

- After passing, he cuts hard across the lane and uses the double screen set by O4 and O5

O2

- Stays spaced from O1, and then O4, when he receives the ball

- Sets himself up for a kick-out pass and three-point shot, if X2 helps

O3 (your best one-on-one player)

- Begins in the opposite low post

- Uses the screen set by O5 and flashes to the ball-side elbow

- Receives a pass from O1, squares up and looks for O1 coming off the double screen

- As the side clears, he goes one-on-one with his defender

04

- L-cuts to get open on the wing, receives entry pass and pitches the ball back to 01

- After handing the ball back to 01, he cuts across the key to set a double with 05

05

- Starts in the middle of the foul line

- Sets a diagonal screen for 03 as 01 is cutting behind 04 for the pitch-back

- Remains on the weakside block, setting a double screen with 04

PITCH-BACK TO SCREEN-AND-ROLL

Diagram 37

Diagram 38

01

- Enters the ball to 03 on the wing

- Follows the pass for a pitch-back from 03

- As 03 is clearing and coming off the down screen from 04, 01 begins to execute a screen-and-roll play with 05

- 01 dribbles off the ball screen set by 05 and looks to attack the basket off the dribble, or

    —Feeds the ball to 05 rolling to the basket

    —Hits 02 for three-pointer if his man sags and helps

—Hits O3 coming off the down screen set by O4

—Passes to O4, who opens up to the ball after he has set the down screen for O3

O2

- Stays spaced 15–17 feet from O1

- As O1 goes to the ball for the pitch-back, O2 fades to the weak side, spotting up for a three-point shot if his defender sags to help on the drive

- Stays spaced behind O1, coming off the ball screen set by O5 and O3, who is coming off a down screen set by O4

O3

- Makes an L-cut from the ball-side block up the lane to get open on the wing

- Receives the entry pass from O1

- Squares to the basket and executes a pitch-back play with O1

- After the pitch-back, O3 cuts to the basket and through the lane to use a down screen set by O4 on the opposite block

- Looks for a pass from O1 as he comes off of O4's down screen

O4

- Begins on the weakside block

- Steps out to time his down screen for O3, as he cuts through the lane and off of the screen

- After screening, he opens to the ball if his defender cheats, or after a solid screen has been set

O5

- Begins in the middle of the foul line

- Times his on-the-ball screen for O1 with the pitch-back from O3

- Sets a solid ball screen for O1

- After screening for O1, he opens to the ball and rolls to the basket, looking for a return pass from O1

DRIBBLE-PULL ISOLATION FOR CENTER

Dribble pull is a term used to describe when one player dribbles toward another player, causing the player being dribbled at to clear the area. The example in this diagram is 01 dribbling toward 03 and 03 clearing that side of the floor.

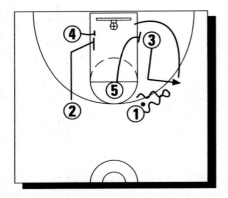

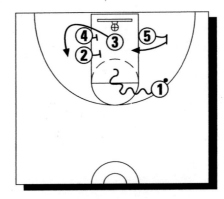

Diagram 39   **Diagram 40**

01

- Dribbles at 03, moving him out of the wing area and off the double screen set by 04 and 05

- After dribbling toward 03 and clearing him out, 01 reverses his dribble and goes hard toward the middle of the floor

- He looks to attack the basket or hit 03, who is coming off the double screen on the opposite side of the floor

- This motion pulls the defense hard toward the direction that the ball is moving

- 01 then reverses again and feeds 05, who has stepped into the lane and posted hard, calling for the ball

- 01 then has the following options:

  —Continue to attack the basket with the dribble

  —Hit 03 coming off the double screen

  —Feed 05 ducking hard into the lane

  —Fee either 02 or 04, who can slip their screen if their defender overplays and cheats toward the play

02
- As O1 dribbles out toward O3, he cuts hard to the weakside block to set a double screen for O3

- Looks to slip the screen and cut to the basket if his man cheats and overplays the play

03
- Makes an L cut from the ball-side block, up the lane, to get open on the wing

- As O1 dribbles toward him, he cuts hard toward the lane

- First, he goes off O5's screen, and then he goes off the double screen as O1 reverses his dribble

- Looks for the pass from O1 as he curls off the double screen

04
- Begins on the weakside block

- Steps out so he can time the double screen for O3 as he cuts through the lane and off the double

- Opens up to the ball as the cutter goes by the screen, and basket cuts if his defender overplays O3 as he curls off the double

05
- Begins in the middle of the foul line

- Cuts to the ball-side block as O1 begins his dribble pull toward O3

- Sets a solid back screen for O3 as he clears the ball side

- After O3 clears his line of vision, he ducks in hard, looking for the pass from O1

DRIBBLE DOUBLE ISOLATION

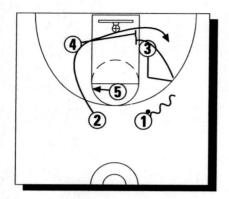

Diagram 41

Diagram 42

O1

- Dribbles to the wing, pushing O3 down to the block

- His reads are as follows:

    —O4 in the post

    —O2 coming off the double

    —O3 in the high post

    —O5, if his man sags to help

O2

- Cuts hard off the double screen set by O3 and O4

- If not open, he spots up in the corner for an open three or post feed to O3

O3

- Drops to the post for a double screen or dribble move by O1

- Is the top man in the double screen

- As soon as O2 clears the double and O4 flashes high, he posts hard

- Reads how he is being played and seals the defender off; he can be fed from any position

04

- As 01 dribbles to the wing, he crosses the lane and is the bottom man on the double

- Sets the double with 03 and, as soon as 02 clears the screen, he flashes high

- Looks to receive for a shot or a high-low to 03 in the low post

05

- Starts at the foul line and flashes out to the opposite wing as 01 dribbles down

- Makes himself available for a shot or high-low to 03

TWO CUTTERS—HIGH POST SPLIT

High post split is a term used to describe two players alternately "X" cutting off the man in the high post

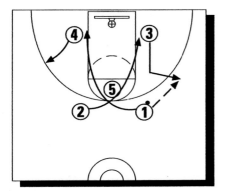

Diagram 43   **Diagram 44**

01

- Enters the ball to 03, who has cut to the wing

- Is the second cutter off the high post split screen

- Cuts hard to the weakside block

- Sets his man up to receive a down screen from 04

- Looks to receive a pass from 05 for a shot or a post feed to 04, who has just set the screen for him

02

- Is the first cutter to split the post

- He may cut above or below the high post screen, depending on how his defender plays the split cut

- Cuts hard to the ball-side block, looking for a pass from 04

- If the ball is passed to 05, he set his man up, reads the defender, and comes off a down screen set by 03

- Looks to receive the pass from 05 and can either shoot or look to feed the ball to 03 in the post

03

- L-cuts to get open on the wing

- Receives the entry pass from 01 and squares up, looking to feed the ball to either cutter coming off the high post split

- If neither cutter is open, he reverses the ball to 05 and sets a down screen for 02, who is setting his man up at the low post

- After screening down hard, he posts up hard and calls for the ball

- Looks for a post feed from either 02 on the wing or 05 in the high post

- If the defense overplays the down screen, he can look to slip the screen and make a cut to the basket

04

- As the ball is entered to 03, he steps to the wing to open up the post area for the first two cutters and improve his angle for the down screen he is going to set

- Sets a solid down screen for 01 as soon as the ball is reversed to 05 in the high post area

- Looks to post up after setting a solid down screen for 01

- Could receive a post feed from 05 on the high post reversal or, if the ball is swung, from 01 on the wing

- If the defense overplays the down screen, he can look to slip the screen and make a direct cut to the basket

O5

- Begins in the middle of the foul line

- As the ball is entered to the wing, he sets a solid screen for the first cutter (O2) as he goes to the basket

- Next, he turns and screens for the second cutter (O1)

- After screening for both cutters, he steps back to receive a pass from O3

- The better screen he sets for the cutters, the more likely his man will have to hedge out and help on the cutters, making it easier for him to be open for the pass from O3

- Options are

    —Pass to O1 coming off the down screen

    —Feed to O4, who has just set the down screen and is posting up

    —Pass to O2 coming off the down screen on the other side

    —Feed to O3, who has just set the down screen for O2 and is posted up

TWO CUTTERS, HIGH POST SPLIT TO TRIANGLES

This play is a continuation of the previous play that we call the *Two-Cutter series.* The diagrams will begin with the ball in the hands of O5 at the high post and with players O1 and O2 coming off the down screens. This series uses the principle of screening the screener.

Diagram 45

Diagram 46

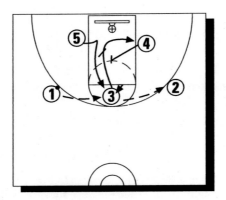

Diagram 47

01 (Diagram 45)

- Catches the ball on the wing from 05

- Squares and looks for the following options:

    —04 posting up strong in the low post ball side

    —03 coming off the diagonal down screen set by 05

    —05 coming off the cross screen set by 04

- On any pass that goes to either the high post or the low post, 01 relocates on the perimeter and spots up for a kick-out pass and a shot

- If the first pass goes from 05 to 02 (Diagram 46), he stays spaced and clear of the high post area and readies himself for a reversal pass from the player just entering the high post

02

- If the ball is passed to him from 05 instead of to 01, he would assume all the same responsibilities and reads that were described above for 01 (Diagram 46)

- If he does not receive the pass from 05, he stays spaced and clear of the high post area

- Readies himself for a potential reversal pass from the player just entering the high post

03 (Diagram 45)

- Looks to receive a post pass from 05

- If the ball is reversed away, O3 steps off and out of the lane to create a better angle to receive the diagonal screen

- He sets his man up by "V" cutting to the basket, and cuts hard off the shoulder of the diagonal screener coming down from the high post

- Coming off the diagonal screen, he fills the high post area for a shot or a high-low pass

- If he doesn't have an open shot, his options are as follows:

    —Feed O5 for a post-up after the diagonal down screen

    —Feed O5 coming off O4's cross screen

    —Feed O4, who has opened to the ball after setting the cross screen

    —Reverse the ball to O2

O4 (Diagram 45)
- Posts up hard, looking for a pass from O1

- If he cannot seal his man, he rolls out to set a cross screen for O5

- After setting the cross screen, he opens up right away, looking for a high-low feed

O5 (Diagram 45)
- Tries to reverse the ball from the previous wing from which it came

- Takes a step toward the ball to move the defender and then sets a diagonal down screen for O3 on the opposite block; after screening, he opens to the ball

- If the ball is not passed to him, he must immediately step out of the lane to set himself up for O4's cross screen

- If O5 reads the defender, he can go either above or below the cross screen and post up, asking for the ball from either O1 or O3

If no one in the triangle is open, the ball is reversed and the action starts all over again (Diagram 47).

TWO-CUTTER TO FIVE-MAN DIAGONAL SCREEN—
DOWN SCREEN/CROSS SCREEN

Note: This play is another continuation option of the two-cutter plays. The diagrams pick up the play after the ball has been passed back to O5 at the high post and O3 and O4 have screened down for O1 and O2.

Diagram 48

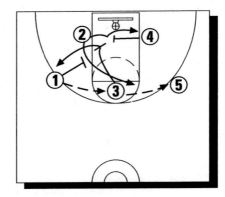

Diagram 49

O1

- Catches the ball from O5 and squares up

- His reads are as follows:

  —O4 posting up

  —O3 coming to the high post area off a diagonal screen set by O5

  —If O3 were covered, then O1 would next look for O2 coming off O4's cross screen

O2

- Sets a down screen for O5 and looks for the ball

- Receives a cross screen from O4

- If the ball has already been reversed, or if O2 does not get the ball, he must quickly step off of the lane and get ready to receive a diagonal screen from the player at the high post

O3

- As the ball is reversed, O3 comes off a diagonal screen from O5 and cuts to the high post area

- As 03 catches the ball, he has the following reads:

  —Looks to 05, who has just screened for him

  —Looks for 02, who is down screening for 05 and then posting

  —Looks to 04, who is receiving a cross screen from 02

  —Looks to reverse the ball to 05 on the wing

- After he reverses the ball, the rotation will continue and 03 looks to make a diagonal screen again for 02

04

- Posts hard as soon as the ball is thrown to the wing

- As soon as he has received the ball, 04 rolls out to set a cross screen for 02, who has just screened down

- When the ball is reversed, the continuity keeps going

05

- Reverses the ball to 01 on the wing

- Starts toward the ball and then sets a diagonal screen for 03, who is on the opposite block

- 05 then looks to post for a count and then comes off a down screen from 02 on the wing

- 05 then looks to receive the reversal pass and looks inside

- If nothing is open in the post area, 05 reverses the ball to the point and the whole process starts over again

LOB-AND-CENTER ISOLATION

Diagram 50

Diagram 51

O1

- Enters the ball to O3 and follows for a pitch-back

- First look is to O5, who has cut into the low post and is isolated

- Second look is for the lob to O3 circling off the back screen set by O4

- Then he looks back to O5 and reads how he is being defended:

    —If he is being played behind, O1 can make a direct pass

    —If he is being fronted, O1 can go to O4 for he high-low or loft a pass over the defender

    —If the defense on O5 has been caught on top, then he can go to O2 in the corner for the post feed

O2

- On the entry pass to O3, he makes a hard cut to the ball-side corner

- He spots up for a three or can prepare to feed the post if his defender is on top

O3

- Receives the entry pass and pitches the ball back to O1

- Delays slightly to set up his cut and wait for O4 to set the back screen

- Comes off the back screen, looking for a lob from O1, and then clears to open the post

04

- Fills the high post as 05 vacates and sets a back screen for 03

- Reads how 05 is being played and prepares to make a high-low pass

05

- As the ball is entered to 03, he cuts hard into the low post and allows the defense to establish the defensive position; 05 then seals his defender off and expects the pass from the correct perimeter player

WEAKSIDE SPLIT

Diagram 52

01

- Enters the ball to 03 on the wing

- Stays spaced and ready to receive the reversal if none of the cutters are open

02

- As the ball is entered to 03, he jab steps toward 01 and then makes a hard cut on the weak side of 05 to the corner

- Attempts to rub his man off on 05 by cutting shoulder to shoulder

03

- L-cuts up to the wing to get open

- Catches and squares, looking first to 02 cutting on the back side of 05

- Second look is to 04 cutting over the top of 05 and down to the ball-side block

04

• Pops out to the wing as the ball is entered to 03

• Becomes the second cutter off 05, going over the top and curling down to the ball-side block

05

• As the ball is entered, he moves to the elbow opposite

• Searches for defenders to screen

• Looking first for X2 and then X4, trying with both to get solid contact

WEAKSIDE SPLIT—CONTINUED

Diagram 53

This play begins with the players in the positions they were in when the previous play ended (Diagram 52).

01

• Has maintained spacing with 03 and pops back toward the ball to receive a reversal pass

• Swings the ball to 05 and stays spaced

02

• As the ball is swung back to 05, he sets up his defender and cuts over the top of 04

• As he cuts, he tries to get a piece of X3 to help 03 get open

• He cuts hard to the ball-side elbow, calling for the ball

03

- Hits 01 as he pops to get open and sets his man up by stepping in the direction of the pass

- As 05 catches the reversal from 01, 03 cuts hard under 04's screen, looking for the pass from 05

04

- As the ball is swung to 01, he steps up and targets the ball to occupy his defender

- As 05 catches the ball, he steps out from the key and sets a back screen first for 02 splitting over the top and then for 03 going underneath

05

- After setting the screen in the previous play, he steps out and receives the reversal pass from 01, looking first for 02 cutting toward the ball-side elbow and then for 03 cutting under 04 toward the ball-side block

TRIPLE SPLIT

Diagram 54

01

- Enters the ball to 03 and moves toward 02, attempting to get a brush screen on X2

- After waiting for 02 and 04 to cut split off 05, he cuts off the back screen set by 05

- As he cuts down the lane, he cuts off 04's screen in the ball-side low post and goes hard to the corner, looking for the pass and the jumper or the post feed

O2

- Sets up his man by going away from the direction of the entry pass and then cutting hard first off O1's screen and then off O5's screen

- If he does not receive the pass on his cut, he circles out to the weak side and up to the top as a release man

O3

- L-cuts to get open on the wing

- Reads the three cutters as they split off O5

- First to O2 cutting over the top, then to O4 also cutting over the top, then to O1 cutting off the weak side of O5 and then underneath O4 at the block to the corner

O4

- Is the second cutter to split off O5, going over the top and posting at the ball-side block

- If he doesn't get a pass on the quick post, he turns and screens for O1 circling to the corner and reestablishes position at the block for a pass from O3 or O1

O5

- Starts in the middle of the foul line and screens first for O2 over the top, then for O4 over the top and then for O1 on the weakside split

BACK CUT AND ISOLATION FOR O3 AT THE BLOCK

This play is also used as a pressure release when the defense overplays the entry pass to O3.

Diagram 55

Diagram 56

01
- Enters the ball to O5 at the high post

- Quickly moves to screen away for O2

- Stays spaced from O5 to prevent his man from sagging

02
- Sets his man up and comes off the screen set by O1

- Uses the screen to move to the area vacated by O1, staying spaced and ready for a kick-out from O5

03
- L-cuts hard to get open, then plants and makes a straight-line backdoor cut, looking for the bounce pass from O5

- Stops at the post to screen for O4 cutting to the corner

- Then he attempts to step hard over his defender, into the lane, looking for the high-low pass from O5

- If his man helps on O4's cut or gets caught on the baseline or front side, he should be able to seal him off and receive the pass from O5

- If his man denies the high-low pass by being on top, he seals him off and looks for ball to be skipped to O4 in the corner

- O4 should have a good passing angle if he has sealed his defender on his top side

04
- Waits to cut until he is sure that O3 is not going to receive the pass from O5 on the back cut

- Cuts hard off O3 in the block and reads how X3 is playing O3 in the block

- He can expect a pass from O5 to feed O3 if X3 is defending on top

05
- Pops up to the high post to receive the entry pass and looks to throw a bounce pass to the back-cutting O3, lets O4 cut off O3 and reads the defense to see if he can make a high-low pass

- If he sees that the defender on O3 is playing on the top and denying a direct pass, he skips the ball to O4 in the corner and anticipates that he will feed O3 in the low post

- Moves to the weakside offensive rebounding position

CIRCLE THROUGH—HIGH POST SPLIT—CRACKDOWN SCREENS

Diagram 57

Diagram 58

Diagram 59

O1

- Enters the ball to O5, goes toward O2 and attempts to get a brush screen on X2

- He is the second cutter to split the post

- When the post has the ball on a post split, the cutters look for either a handoff or a return pass after he has cleared the post

- After splitting the post, he goes to the low post and sets his man up for a *crackdown* screen set by O3, coming from the baseline

- He uses the screen and reads his defender to decide if he is going to curl or fade off the screen

- Comes off ready to shoot or penetrate and drop or feed the new post coming toward him on the cross screen (Diagram 59)

02
- He is the first cutter in the high post split, going as soon as O5 receives the entry pass from O1

- Cuts hard, looking for a handoff or a pass from O5 after he has cleared the high post split

- Goes to the post on the side of his cut and begins to set his man up for the *crackdown* screen from O4

- He reads the screen to decide if he should curl or fade and then comes off looking for a pass, a shot or penetration

- He can also wait for the new post coming off a cross screen (Diagram 59)

03
- L-cuts out and then back cuts looking for a bounce pass from O5

- Circles through to the opposite baseline and waits for the two guards to split the post

- As soon as the guards have established their position on the block, O3 sets a crackdown screen for O1

- As soon as O1 has cleared his line of vision, he steps hard over his defender, looking for a high-low pass from O5

- If the ball goes to O1, he sets a cross screen for O4 and rebounds the weak side (Diagram 59)

- If the ball goes to the guard on the opposite side, he receives the cross screen and posts up (Diagram 59)

04
- Pops out and then back cuts as O5 receives the entry pass from O1

- He circles through to the opposite baseline and waits for the guards to split the post

- After the guards have established themselves at the post, O4 sets a crackdown screen for O2

- After O2 has cleared his line of vision, he steps hard into the key, looking for the high-low pass from O5

- If the ball goes to O2, he sets a cross screen for O3

- If the ball goes to the guard on the opposite side, he receives the cross screen and posts up (Diagram 59)

O5
- Pops up to receive the entry pass from O1

- Takes a quick look for either O3 or O4 on a backdoor cut

- Looks to hand the ball off to either cutter as the guards split the post

- Pivots and faces the basket and watches as O3 and O4 crack down on the guards in the key; he can pass to either guard or either forward stepping over into the key

GUARD AROUND INTO A DOUBLE SCREEN

Diagram 60

Diagram 61

O1
- Enters the ball to O3 and follows his pass all the way around O3 and to the ball-side block

- At the block, he sets up on top of a double screen with O5

- After both cutters have gone off the double screen, he screens down for O5 so he can *pop the stack* (Diagram 62); when two players pop the stack, the top player in the double screens down for the bottom player, who steps in and then over the screener with a quick flash into the key; with the guard on top of the double and setting the screen down for the post, it makes it difficult for the defenders to switch this action

O2

- Moves away as the ball is entered to O3

- Quickly changes direction and moves back toward O3 to receive the reversal pass

- Reads the cutters as they go one over and one under the double screen, hitting either player who is open

- If neither O3 nor O4 is open, he waits for O5 to pop the stack and flash up into the key

- If nothing has opened up, O2 has the freedom to take the ball to the basket on dribble penetration and either score or drop it off

O3

- L-cuts out to the wing to receive the entry pass from O1

- Lets O1 go around him and then reverses the ball back to O2 at the top of the circle

- After passing to O2, he sets his defender up and goes over the top of the double screen set by O1 and O5, looking for a return pass from O2

O4

- Pops out to the perimeter, and then, as the ball is reversed to O2, he sets his man up and goes under the double screen on the opposite block

O5

- Starts in the middle of the foul line, and then, as the ball is entered into O3, he slides down to the block and sets a double screen with O1

- Sets up on the bottom of the double

- As the cutters go off the double screen, he steps in to the key and then pops the stack off O1's screen (Diagram 62)

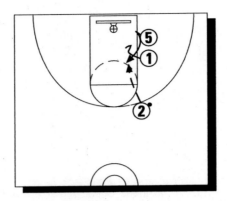

Diagram 62

FRONT CUT FOR THE FORWARDS

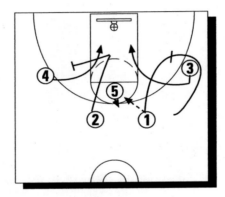

Diagram 63

O1
- Enters the ball directly to O5 at the high post

- Circles on the inside of O3 and looks to get contact with X3 at an angle that O3 can use to front cut to the basket

- Continues his circle back out to his original position

O2
- After the ball has been entered to O5, he takes a hard cut to the basket, trying to beat his defender on a direct cut

- He then circles back to screen for O4 at an angle that O4 can use to front cut off the screen

O3

• As the ball is caught by O5, he starts coming up and then front cuts off O1's screen, looking for a pass from O5 on the basket cut

O4

• After O2 has made his cut and O3 has made his, O4 front cuts over the top of O2's screen, looking for the pass from O5

O5

• Pops out to receive the entry pass

• Turns and looks for O2 on a back cut to the basket

• Turns back to the other side to look for O3 front cutting off O1's screen

• His third look is to O4 cutting off O2's screen

• If nothing is available, he has the freedom to take the ball to the basket on the dribble or reset

BALL SCREEN—SHUFFLE CUT

Diagram 64

O1

• Sets up his dribble angle and comes off O3's ball screen

• Looks to turn the corner and take the ball to the basket

• As he penetrates, if X2 sags to help on the drive, he can kick the ball out to O2 in the corner for the three

• His next look as he drives is for O5, who has set the shuffle screen for O2 and then received a back screen from O4

02

- As O1 dribbles toward O3's ball screen, he runs a shuffle cut off O5's screen

- He cuts hard and quick to the corner and spots up

- If his man sags to help, he should receive a pass from O1 for a three

03

- Moves up toward O1 and sets a ball screen at an angle that allows O1 to turn the corner to the basket; he then pops out to the perimeter

04

- After O5 has set the screen on the shuffle cut, he sets a back screen for O5 to roll to the basket and then pops to the perimeter

05

- As the ball screen is occurring, he sets a screen for O2 to make a shuffle cut

- He immediately receives a back screen from O4 and peels off to the basket, looking for the lob from O1

SHUFFLE CUT TO A BASELINE WEAVE

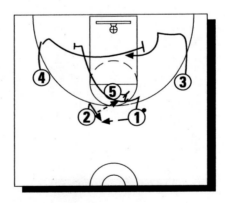

Diagram 65

01

- Reverses the ball to O2 and takes a hard shuffle cut off O5 to the ball-side block

- As O5 receives the ball, he sets a back screen for O4 as he steps out from the block to the perimeter

- Continues in the weave pattern with O4 and O3

O2

- Steps back to the ball to allow O1 to reverse him the ball

- Reads the shuffle cut and gives the ball to O1 if he is open

- If O1 is not open, he passes to O5 stepping out from the screen and keeps spacing

O3

- L-cuts out to the wing and then drops down to the baseline as O5 receives the pass from O2

- Cuts off O4's screen and then sets a screen for O2 as the weave continues

O4

- Pops up to the wing to allow space for O1 to get open on the shuffle cut

- Drops down to the baseline as O5 catches the ball and receives a screen from O1; cuts across the key looking for a pass from O5; and sets a screen for O3 as the weave continues

O5

- Steps out to set the screen for O1 to shuffle cut and then steps out for a pass from O2

- Begins reading the baseline weave, first with O4 coming off a back screen from O1, then with O3 on the screen from O4, and then with O1 off the screen by O3

BACK CUT AND SCREEN THE SCREENER

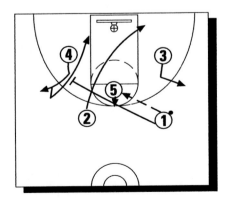

Diagram 66

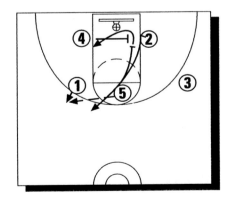

Diagram 67

01

- Enters the ball to 05

- Immediately cuts toward 04, as if he were going to set a screen so 04 could come over the top

- Steps back off the screen and receives the pass from 05, looking either for 02 coming off 05's down screen or for 05 coming to the ball-side post

02

- As soon as 05 catches the ball, he runs a tight back cut, looking for the return pass

- He stops on the far-side block and waits for the ball to be passed to 01

- Sets his man up and comes up off 05's down screen, looking for the shot

03

- Maintains spacing and is ready for a kick-out pass if his man sags to help

04

- As the ball is passed to 05, 04 sets up as if he were going to go over the top of 01's screen and then quickly back cuts to the near-side block

- As 05 swings the ball to 01, he lets 05 screen down and then screens across for 05

05

- Receives the entry pass from 01 and turns quickly to see if 02 is open on the backdoor cut

- Second look is to 04 on a backdoor cut, and then he swings the ball to 01

- After passing, he screens down for 02 on the opposite block

- After screening for 02, he receives a cross screen from 04 and cuts hard to the post

POST HANDOFF AND PENETRATION

Diagram 68

Diagram 69

O1

- Enters the ball to O5 at the high post

- Screens away for O3 to cut toward the high post

- Maintains his spacing

O2

- As the ball is entered to O5, he fades to the corner and spots up, waiting for the penetration and calling for the ball if his man sags to help on the drive

- This play would be run to this side if O2 were the better perimeter shooter of the two guards

O3

- As O5 receives the entry pass, he sets his man up and comes off O1's screen toward the high post

- He gets a handoff from O5 at the high post and looks to turn the corner with the dribble

- He takes it as deep as he can and kicks out to O2 if X2 sags to help, or to O4 if X4 helps on the drive

O4

- As the ball is entered to O5, he back cuts hard to the opposite block and prepares to receive a pass from O3 on penetration if X4 helps on the drive

O5

- Receives the entry pass from O1 and looks backdoor to O4

- He then hands off to O3 cutting over the top of him

SINGLE SCREENS FOR O5 AND O1

Diagram 70   **Diagram 71**

O1

- Enters the ball to O4 flashing hard from the weak side into the high post

- Cuts right off O4, looking to rub his man off and get open after he has passed O4

- Delays in the block until the ball has been passed to O5 and then receives O4's down screen and cuts back to the top of the circle for the shot

O2

- As O4 flashes, O2 cuts hard to the corner and occupies his defender

O3

- As soon as O4 catches and pivots, O3 screens down for O5 at the block and rolls off, looking for a high-low pass

O4

- Flashes into the high post as O5 vacates, catches and looks to hand off or pass to O1 as he cuts by

- Pivots and faces the basket; reads O5 coming off the down screen set by O3

- After passing to O5, he sets a down screen for O1 and opens to the ball

05

• As the ball is being advanced by 01, he slides down to the low post on 03's side

• As 04 pivots and faces the basket, 05 sets up his defender and comes off 03's down screen, looking for a shot or penetration

• If he does not have a shot, he looks for 01 coming off the down screen set by 04

LOB AND ISOLATION FOR THE HIGH POST

In this play, if 04 were our best athlete or the player we wanted to isolate, we would move him into the high post.

Diagram 72

Diagram 73

01

• Reverses the ball to 02 to initiate the action

• If the lob is not there, he V cuts and receives the ball back from 02, takes it around to the side where 04 is posted and works to get an angle to enter the ball to him in the low post

02

• Receives the ball on the reversal, takes one dribble, as if he were going to pass the ball to 03 in the corner, and looks to lob to 04 on the vacated side of the floor

• If the lob is not there, he reverses the ball back to 01

03

• As the ball is passed to 02, he makes a hard cut to the opposite corner, going off 05's screen

04

- Begins in the high post and, as the ball is passed to 02, moves as if he wanted to receive a direct pass from 02 and then quickly spins off and looks for the lob

- If he doesn't receive the lob from 02, he posts hard and waits for 01 to bring the ball to him

05

- Starts on the wing, and, as the ball is passed to 02, he screens in for 03 circling to the corner

- If the lob is not thrown to 04, 05 flashes to the high post for a potential pass from 01 so he can feed 04 on the block

CHAPTER 2

Set Plays to Score from a 1-4 High Set

OVERVIEW OF THE 1-4 HIGH SET

The 1-4 high set provides a team with a potentially quick-hitting attack. It is designed to neutralize half-court pressure. Every pass leads to a scoring opportunity and all the initial cuts are going toward the basket area, where there is no defensive help available. The alignment allows for each of the four players without the ball to be a potential receiver for the entry pass, which creates an unlimited variety of set plays.

As with most sets, it is easy to transfer from the set play into a motion offense or to reset back into the 1-4. But the most significant advantage of the high 1-4 set is its effectiveness against pressuring, overplaying defenses. By setting up with four players across the foul line, the offense has basically taken away any defensive weakside help, and therefore the defense must depend entirely on each defender to pressure the entry and still be able to stop any backdoor cut by himself. Each player is within one pass of the ball, so if any one of the defenders cannot deny the entry pass, the ball can be entered without having to fight the pressure. Even if all the defenders can deny the initial entry pass, if there is one that cannot stop a backdoor cut, the whole defense must then soften up in order to help that one player.

The tighter the defense plays, the more the basket area opens up for drives or cuts. A coach has the ability to use his players' talents to isolate defenders, exploit mismatches and bring larger defenders away from the basket. It can be used as an offense against man, zone or any combination with just a few variations to the movement and reads.

As you will see on the following pages, the 1-4 high set can offer many of the same quick scoring opportunities that were used in our 2-3 set, but with just a little different look.

The #1 man must be the "quarterback" of the offense and understand where the weaknesses of the defense are located and be able to attack them correctly. He will initiate each play with his decision making. Many of the set plays will begin with a ball screen, where the #1 man must be able to read the defense and penetrate, kick the ball out to perimeter players or drop it off to post players.

The wings (#2 and #3) must also be able to move to the point when the offense has to reset. It is essential that they are able to attack the basket with cuts and drives, as well as shoot the perimeter shot. They set up either at the foul line extended or slightly higher if they are pressured. The further they are from the basket, the more difficult it is for the defenders to cover basket cuts.

The post players (#4 and #5) set up on the elbows and are usually interchangeable. They are most effective if they are quick, active athletes who can both pass and attack off the dribble. When playing against taller, slower post players, the biggest mismatch may be found with quicker posts having the ball facing the basket from 15–18 feet.

Most plays from a 1-4 high set begin with hard cuts directly to the basket, either without a screen or by rubbing off one of the posts. It is essential that all plays can be run to either side of the floor so that specific players can be determined on the basis of who receives the entry pass. For example, if the ball goes to the wing, one pattern develops, and if the ball goes to the post, another play is run. The entry pass keys the action that follows. As is the case with all other set plays, it is the speed and execution of the fundamentals that will produce the desired outcome.

1-4 PLAY #1

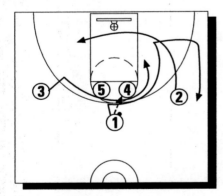 

Diagram 74   **Diagram 75**

01
- Enters the ball to O4 at the right elbow

- V-cuts away from his pass and then cuts hard off O4, looking for a handoff

- If he does not receive the handoff, he circles back out to the wing

02
- As the ball is in the air toward O4, O2 makes a hard back cut to the basket

- He stops at the block and waits for 03 to circle 04 and then for 04 to take a dribble to the middle of the foul line

- He comes up off 05's screen and looks for the shot or post feed to 05

03
- After 02 and 01 have made their cuts, 03 V-cuts away and then curls hard off 04, looking for the handoff and drive

04
- Receives the entry pass and looks over his shoulder to see if 02 is open on the backdoor cut

- Then 01 cuts off him, and 04 will hand the ball off if X1 is behind him

- The third cutter is 03 curling off

- After 03 has passed him, 04 takes a dribble toward the middle of the foul line to improve his passing angle to 02 coming off the down screen set by 05

05
- Starts on the right elbow, and, after all three cutters have passed 04, he turns to the outside and screens down for 02; after screening, he posts up hard

1-4 HIGH SET—PLAY #2

Diagram 76

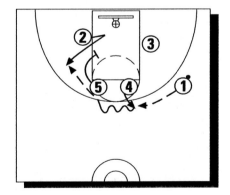

Diagram 77

This play is the same as the previous play, except that it begins with a dribble pull by 01.

01
- Dribbles the ball at 02 on the wing and looks for him to be open on the back cut

- Looks for the second cutter, O3, curling off O4 at the high post

- If neither is open, he hits O4 stepping out from the post

O2
- Makes a basket cut as O1 dribbles toward him and goes through to the opposite block

- Waits for the ball to be reversed to O4 and then comes up off O5's screen, looking for a shot or post feed back to the screener

O3
- As O1 dribbles toward O2, O3 runs a hard curl cut off O4 at the elbow, looking for a pass from O1

O4
- As the ball is dribbled toward O2, O4 sets up to set a screen for O3, curling around him and heading to the basket

- After O3 has cleared the screen, O4 pops out to the top of the circle and receives a reversal pass from O1

- He takes the ball to the far side of the court and reads O2 coming off O5's down screen

O5
- Waits for the ball to be swung to O4 and then turns to the outside and screens down for O2 on the block

- After screening, he posts hard and looks for the pass from O2 or O4

1-4 HIGH SET—PLAY #3

 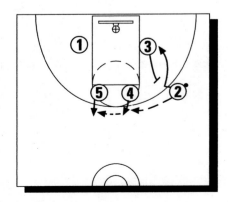

Diagram 78   **Diagram 79**

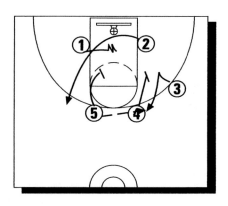

Diagram 80   **Diagram 81**

01

• Enters the ball to 02 and makes a direct cut to the opposite-side block

• He waits until the ball has been reversed through 04 and 05, and then he screens across the key, making the first of a staggered double screen for 02

02

• Receives the entry pass and looks at 03 cutting hard off 05 and coming to the near-side block

• Reverses the ball to 04 and receives a back screen from 03 and cuts to the near block

• As the ball gets swung through 04 and 05, he comes up off a staggered double screen set by 01 and then by 05

• If he catches the ball and doesn't have a shot, he looks back to 03, who is using a back screen set by 04

03

• As the ball is entered to 02, 03 takes a hard curl cut off 05 and goes to the ball-side block

• As the ball is reversed to 04, he sets a back screen for 02 and moves up so he is even with the level of the ball

• As 02 catches the ball, 03 will receive a down screen from 04 and come up to receive the ball from 05

• After catching the ball, he reads 02 coming off the staggered double screen

- After hitting O2, O3 receives a back screen from O4 and goes to the basket

O4
- After O3 has curled to the basket, O4 pops out to catch a reversal pass from O2

- As he catches the ball, he looks first to O2 going off O3's back screen

- If O2 is not open, he swings the ball to O5 and moves down to set a screen for O3 to pop up

- As O2 receives the ball from O5 off the staggered double screen, O4 sets the back screen for O3 to cut to the basket

O5
- Sets the screen for O3 curling to the basket and then pops up even with the top of the circle

- He is looking for a reversal pass from O4; after receiving it, he swings it right back to O3 and sets the second part of the staggered double screen with O1 so O2 can get open for the perimeter shot

- This play offers multiple opportunities to score:

    —O3 on the curl cut

    —O2 on the back screen

    —O2 on the staggered double

    —O3 on the back screen

1-4 HIGH SET— PLAY #4

Diagram 82

Diagram 83

Diagram 84

01

- Enters the ball to O2 on the wing and takes a hard rub cut off O4 at the high post

- If he can rub his defender off on O4, he should get the ball early and attack the basket

- He waits on the block until the ball is swung to O5 and then receives a down screen from O4 and cuts to the wing for a shot

- If he does not have a shot when he catches on the wing, he first reads O4 posting up after screening for him and then O3 coming off a staggered double on the far side

02

- Catches the entry pass from O1 and reads his rub cut off O4

- Looks to O3 in the corner, but then reverses the ball to O5

- As O5 swings the ball to O1, O2 sets the first screen of the staggered double for O3

03

- As the ball is in the air on the way to O2, he takes a quick hard cut to the opposite corner and spots up for a three

- After the ball has been reversed all the way around to O1, he comes off the staggered double screen set by O2 and O5

04

- As the ball is passed to O2 on the wing, he sets a screen for O1 to rub off

- Some coaches prefer to have the post set this kind of screen by turning his back to the cutter and facing the basket so that he can see what his defender is doing to help on the cut—and so the post doesn't do anything to exaggerate his position and get called for a foul

- After O1 has cleared the screen, O4 goes across the foul line and screens for O5

- As the ball gets reversed to O5, he goes down into the key and screens for O1

- After screening for O1, he posts hard and calls for the ball

O5
- After both O3 and O1 have made their first cuts, O5 receives a screen from O4 and cuts toward the ball to receive a reversal pass from O2

- After catching, he swings the ball to O1 coming off the down screen and moves away and sets the second screen on the staggered double for O3

1-4 HIGH SET—PLAY #5

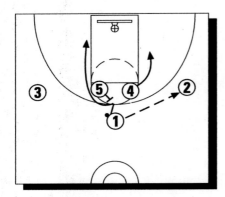

Diagram 85

Diagram 86

Diagram 87

01

- Enters the ball to 02, sets his defender up and cuts off of 05's back screen, looking for the lob from 02

- Holds on the low block opposite until the ball has been swung to 05 and then comes off of 03's down screen

- As he catches the pass on the wing, his first look is to 04 coming across the key off of 03's screen

- Second look is to 03 coming to the top of the circle off of 05's down screen

- This setup is another way to use the principle of screening the screener

02

- Receives the entry pass and looks first to 04 cutting straight down to the block and posting up

- His second look is to 01 cutting off 05's back screen for the lob

- He then reverses the ball back to 05 stepping out from the screen and stays spaced on the perimeter for a kick-out

03

- As the ball is reversed to 05, 03 screens down for 01 on the block, and as he catches it, 03 continues across the key and screens for 04

- After screening for 04, 03 receives a down screen from 05 and cuts back toward the top of the circle for a three

04

- As the ball is entered to 02 on the wing, he slides directly down the ball-side post and works to get the ball; there should not be any help on the post at this time

- As the ball is reversed back to 01, 04 sets up his man and comes off 03's cross screen to the ball-side low post again

05

- As the ball is entered to 02, 05 steps out to set a back screen for 01

- His man should have to hedge off and help on this cut, which allows him to be open for a reversal pass from 02

- As he catches the pass from 02, he looks for 01 coming off the down screen

- After passing to O1, O5 sets a down screen for O3 in the middle of the key

1-4 HIGH SET—PLAY #6

Diagram 88

Diagram 89

O1
- Dribbles at O2, pushing him to the corner

- When he gets to the wing, O5 should be coming off O4's screen and cutting to the ball-side block

- If O5 is not open, O1 reverses the ball back to O4 at the top of the circle and spaces to the perimeter for a kick-out three

O2
- As O1 dribbles toward him, he slides down to the corner and spots up

- As the ball is being reversed to O4, O2 runs a flex cut off O5 across the key, looking for the pass from O4; he can go all the way to the wing to get open

- As he catches the ball on the wing, he has O5 coming to the block and O3 coming up off of O4's down screen

O3
- As the ball is reversed to O4, he crosses the key and sets a screen for O5 to post, and then receives a down screen from O4

O4
- As the ball is dribbled to the wing, he crosses the foul line and screens for O5 to roll to the block

- He steps out from the screen to catch the reversal pass from O1 and hit O2 on the flex cut, or as he clears to the wing

- After passing to O2, he sets a down screen for O3 in the key

O5
- Receives the cross screen from O4 and rolls hard down the lane to the block

- As the ball is swung to O2, he will receive a screen from O3 and again cut to the ball-side block, looking for a post feed from O2

1-4 HIGH SET—PLAY # 7

Diagram 90

Diagram 91

O1
- Uses the same dribble pull action as on the previous play, but this time, O2 curls under O4 and back to the top for the reversal

- As he is dribbling to the wing, his first look is to O4 sliding down the lane after O2 has cleared his screen

- O1 then reverses the ball and relocates on the perimeter

O2
- As O1 dribbles at him, he moves toward O4 and curls under him and tries to brush screen X4 before popping out to the top of the circle

- When he catches the reversal pass from O1, he looks for a high-low to O4 and then to O3 coming off O5's down screen

O3
- As O2 is curling to the top for the reversal, he takes his man down into the key and sets him up for a down screen from O5

- Coming off the down screen, he can shoot or post feed to O5 isolated in the post or go to O4 flashing up to the elbow for a high-low post pass

O4
- After O2 has curled under him, he rolls to the block and posts

- If he does not receive the ball, he waits until the ball has been swung to O3 and then flashes to the ball-side elbow for a shot or a high-low post feed to O5

O5
- As the ball is reversed to O2, he turns to the outside and down screens for O3

- After screening, he posts and seals, looking for a pass from O3 or O4

1-4 HIGH-LOW SET—PLAY #8

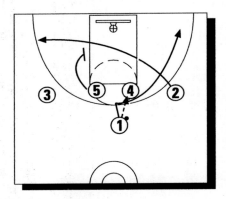

Diagram 92   **Diagram 93**

O1
- Enters the ball to O4 at the elbow and makes a hard cut off O4, looking for a handoff

- Goes to the corner and spots up, waiting for the dribble penetration by O3

O2
- On the entry pass to O4, he cuts directly across the lane off O5's screen to the opposite corner

O3
- Curls over the top of O4 as he takes a dribble in his direction

- Receives the handoff and attempts to turn the corner to the basket

- As he turns the corner, he reads where any defensive help is coming from and either kicks the ball to O1 in the corner or to O5 on the opposite block, if he can't drive all the way to the basket

O4
- Receives the entry pass and looks to handoff to O1 cutting off to the corner

- Pivots back to the middle and takes a hard dribble and looks to hand off to O3 cutting around him

- O4 has the option of going to O2 in the corner or O5 in the post, instead of handing off

O5
- Slides out of the high post to the opposite block as the ball is entered

- He sets a screen for O2 cutting through to the corner and then posts up, looking for a pass from O4

- As O3 penetrates, O5 readies himself for a drop-off pass if his defender helps

1-4 HIGH SET—PLAY # 9—LOOKING FOR A THREE-POINT SHOT

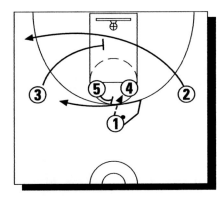

Diagram 94

Diagram 95

O1
- Enters the ball to O4 at the elbow

- V-cuts away and then comes off O5's screen, flaring to the wing and looking for a three

O2
- As the ball is entered to O4, he runs a hard backdoor cut, looking for the pass

- He crosses the key and comes off 03's screen and goes all the way to the corner, looking for a three

03
- As the ball is entered, he goes down into the key and sets a screen for 02

- After screening, he continues on to the far wing and spots up for a three

04
- Receives the entry pass, and his first look is to 02 on a backdoor cut

- Second look is to 01 flaring for a three

- Third look is to 02 in the corner for a three

- Fourth look is to 05 slicing down the key after screening for 01

- Final look is to the opposite side for 03 stepping out to the three-point line after screening for 02

05
- After 01 enters the ball to 04, he steps up and screens 01 at an angle that allows him to get open on a flare cut to the three-point line

- After screening, he rolls off the screen and slices down the center of the lane

1-4 HIGH SET—PLAY #10

Note: This play takes advantage of teams that switch ball screens, forcing them into a "big-little" switch.

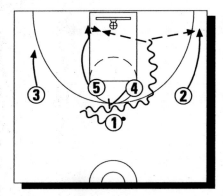

Diagram 96

Diagram 97

Diagram 98

O1

- Dribbles to his left to set a change of direction and be able to come off O4's ball screen

- Reverses his dribble and uses O4's screen

- If he can turn the corner, he can penetrate and either pitch to O2 or drop off to O5 on the opposite block (Diagram 96)

- If he cannot turn the corner, he kicks the ball back to O4 and screens down for O2

- After screening, he relocates back out on the perimeter, spotting up for a three-point shot

O2

- As the ball screen is being set at the top of the circle, O2 slides down to the corner, preparing for O1 to penetrate and pitch (Diagram 96)

- If O1 passes the ball back to O4, he sets up his man and comes off a down screen set by O1 and looks for a three

- If he catches the ball and doesn't have an unguarded shot, he can pass to O3, who is stepping out to the three-point line after screening

- He also has O5 posted up on the ball-side block

O3

- Stays on his side and moves to keep in vision for a potential skip pass for a three-point shot

04

- Steps off the elbow and up to set a ball screen for 01 as he reverses his dribble

- After screening, he reads how the defense has played the ball screen and steps back for a possible return pass from 01

- If the ball comes back to him, he looks first to 03 and a skip pass and then back to 02 coming off 01's down screen

- He also has 05 in the low post ,who should be targeting the ball as it is being swung

05

- After 04 steps up to the top of the circle, 05 slides down to the low block on his side of the key

- He stays there if 01 gets penetration, looking for a drop-off pass if his man helps on the drive

- If 01 passes back to 04, 05 steps across the key to the other block and posts up for a pass from 04, 02, or 01

CHAPTER 3

Set Plays out of Box and Stack Sets

OVERVIEW OF THE BOX SET

The box set uses almost the exact opposite principles as the 1-4 high set. It initially places your players close to the basket and allows the defense to start in the middle of the key. The opposite of the 1-4 high set, the box set is more of a power offense, and most of your first cuts involve moving away from the basket. A coach may choose to run set plays from the box when he has stronger, slower post players and/or shooters whom he wants to bring off screens and pop to the perimeter.

The box set provides good angles and distances to screen, since the defenders are all crowded into the key area. In many ways, the plays run from the box are similar to out-of-bounds plays that start in a tight formation and then move to the perimeter. Keeping the players in tight also provides offensive rebounding opportunities for bigger, slower post players.

Another difference is that your point guard is going to make most of the decision making that leads to shots. He will often make the entry pass that leads directly to a shot or dribble enter the ball to the wing. It is essential that he can handle pressure, because, in most cases, he is isolated either at the point or the wing.

OVERVIEW OF THE STACK SET

A "stack" set is usually begun with two or three player standing together, or two groups of two. They can both be at the elbows or the low post, or they can be staggered. Just by its alignment, it exaggerates the defensive team to one area of the floor and allows the offense to isolate individual players and exploit the defense. Stacking players allows screening to take place with a small amount of movement, which makes it easier to make entry passes that require timing. Stacks provide quick-hitting isolations and shots. Stack sets are often used against both zone and man-to-man, because they create immediate overload situations.

All the following plays from both the stack and the box sets can be adjusted to start players 01, 02, 03 and 04 at any of the positions. This flexibility provides the coach with an opportunity to run plays to get shots for specific individuals or from specific places on the floor. Quick-hitting attacks out of box and stack sets also exploit teams that switch all screens. A coach can set up situations that can create "little to big" switches on the very first cut by calling the correct play. When you look at the following plays, think about the personnel on your team and where you can place them to take advantage of their strengths and avoid their weaknesses.

BOX SET—PLAY #1

Diagram 99

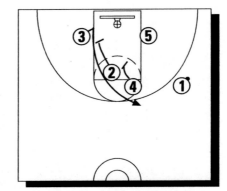

Diagram 100

Diagram 101

O1

- Dribbles toward the wing, outside of O4

- Reads O5 coming down to the block off O2's screen

- Second read is O3 coming toward him off a staggered double screen

- Third read is O4 for a lob off O2's back screen

- During this entire read, O1 wants to keep his dribble alive as he is making his reads

O2

- Starts on the low block on the same side as O4

- As the ball is dribbled to the wing, he makes a diagonal screen up to O5

- After setting the screen for O5, he turns back and down screens for O3 in the first of the staggered double

O3

- Starts on the block below O5

- Comes off the staggered double screen set by O2 and O4

O4

- Starts on the elbow above O2

- Waits for O3 to come off O2's screen and then also screens for him as the second part of the staggered double screen

- After screening for O3, he receives a back screen from O2 and comes off, looking for the lob from O1

O5

- Starts on the elbow away from the direction of the dribble

- As the ball reaches the free throw line extended, he receives a diagonal back screen from O2 and cuts hard to the ball-side block; he is the first option

BOX SET—PLAY #2

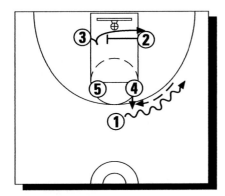

Diagram 102

Diagram 103

01

- Dribbles the ball toward the right wing

- Reads 03 coming to the block off 02's cross screen

- If he has a good passing angle, he makes the post feed

- If 03 is fronted, he reverses the ball to 04 for a high-low entry to the post

02

- Screens away for 03 as the ball is entered on the dribble

- Receives a down screen from 05 to cut to the perimeter for a shot

03

- As the ball is dribbled to the wing, he receives a cross screen from 02

- Comes to the post and seals his defender, whichever side he is being played

- Isolates at the block for either a direct feed from 01 or a high-low from 04

04

- Reads how 03 is being played and pops out with timing so 01 can reverse the ball to him

- Looks for a high-low to 03, to 02 coming off the down screen or 05 rolling off the screen

05

- As the ball is being reversed to 04, 05 screens down for 02 (i.e., screens the screener)

- After screening, he rolls and opens to the ball, looking for a high-low pass from 04 or an entry from the wing from 02

BOX SET—PLAY #3

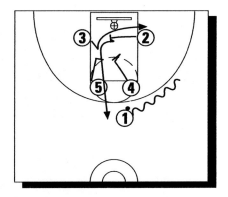

Diagram 104   **Diagram 105**

O1
- Enters the ball to the wing with a dribble

- Reads O3 coming to the block off the cross screen

- If he is not open, his next look is to O2 coming off a double to the three-point line

- Then he looks back to O3 isolated in the low post

- If he is being played on the high side, O4 can enter the ball from the corner

- If he is being fronted, O5 can enter from the elbow

O2
- Screens across for O3 and receives a double screen from O4 and O5

O3
- Receives O2's cross screen and posts up hard

- Relaxes for a second if he doesn't get the initial pass, and then he reseals his defender and can get a pass from O4 in the corner or a high-low from O5 from the elbow

O4
- Sets the double screen with O5 or O2, then cuts hard to the corner, looking to receive a pass and feed O3 isolated in the post

05

- Sets the double screen with 04 for 02 and then cuts quickly to the ball-side elbow, looking to receive a pass and feed 03 if he is fronted

BOX SET—PLAY #4

Diagram 106

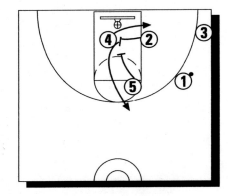

Diagram 107

01

- Enters the ball to the wing with the dribble

- Looks for 02 briefly at the block

- As 03 sprints to the corner, 04 comes off 05's back screen, looking for the lob

- The next read is for 04 coming to the block and then 02 cutting to the top of the circle off 05's down screen

02

- Briefly posts as 04 is going for the lob and then screens for 04

- Receives a down screen from 05 and cuts to the three-point line

03

- As the ball is dribbled to the wing, he cuts hard to the corner to clear the back side for the lob to 04

- Can post feed from the corner if 04 is being played on the high side

04

- As the ball is dribbled to the wing, he peels off 05's back screen, looking for the lob

- If he is not open, he receives a screen from 02 and posts up hard

05

- As the ball gets to the wing, he sets a back screen for 04

- After 04 has cleared the key, he sets a down screen for 02

BOX SET—PLAY #5

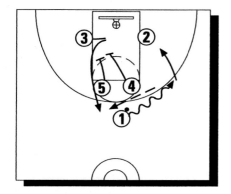

Diagram 108

Diagram 109

01

- Dribbles to the wing and looks for 03 coming off the double screen set by 04 and 05

- Reverses the ball to 03 and basket cuts, looking for a return pass

02

- As the ball is dribbled to the wing, 02 sets his man up, waits for the second double screen set by 04 and 05 and cuts to the wing looking for a three

03

- Starts on the block opposite the dribble entry

- Receives the first double screen from 04 and 05 and cuts to the point, looking for the three

- If he receives the ball and does not have a shot, he looks back to 01 running a give-and-go cut to the basket

- Second look is to 02 coming to the wing off another double set by 04 and 05

O4 and O5

- Time their double screen with the dribble entry

- First double is set for O3 cutting to the top of the circle

- Clear the key and then set the second double for O2 cutting toward the wing looking for the three

- Anticipate the three-point shot and get offensive rebounding position

BOX SET—PLAY #6

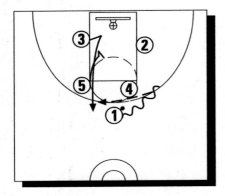

Diagram 110

Diagram 111

O1

- Enters the ball with a dribble to the wing

- Reverses the ball to O3 coming up off O5's screen

- Immediately sets a double screen with O4 on O2

O2

- Posts as the ball is dribbled to his side

- As the ball is swung to O3, O2 sets his man up and comes off a double screen set by O1 and O4, going to the top of the circle for a three

O3

- As the ball is dribbled to the wing, he comes up off a down screen set by O5

- The ball is passed to him from O1, and he takes the ball down to improve his passing angle to O5, who is posting on the block

- As he dribbles down attempting to feed 05, 02 is coming up off a double screen

04
- As the ball is reversed from 01 to 03, he and 01 go down and set a double screen for 02

05
- As the ball is being dribbled to the wing, he sets a down screen for 03

- After screening, he posts and tries to seal the defender on his high side so that 03 has a good feeding angle as 03 dribbles the ball down to the wing

STACK SET—PLAY #1

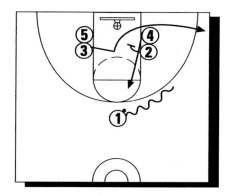

Diagram 112   **Diagram 113**

01
- Dribbles the ball to the right wing

- Reads 03 going to the corner off the double screen set by 02 and 04 in the stack

- 04 pops the stack to the high post, and 05 is coming to the block off the cross screen set by 02

- 05 can be fed by 01, 03 or 04 when he gets isolated in the post

- If 05 is not open, 02 will be coming up off a down screen set by 04

02
- Stacks on the high side of 04; as 03 clears the stack, he screens down on X4

- Next, he crosses the key to screen for 05 and then receives a down screen from 04

03
- As the ball is dribbled to the wing, 03 makes a quick cut to the corner off 02 and 04 in a stack

- Looks to receive the ball from 01 and feed 05 in the post

04
- After 03 clears the stack, 04 pops the stack to the high post to feed 05 if he is fronted

- If the ball cannot be passed to 05, 04 down screens for 02

05
- Waits for 03 to get to the corner and then comes off a cross screen set by 02 (little-to-big switch)

- Seals his defender and looks to be fed from the corner, wing or high post

STACK SET—PLAY #2

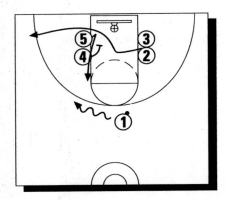

Diagram 114

Diagram 115

01
- Dribble enters the ball to the left wing, away from 02 and 03

- Looks for 02 coming off the double set by 04 and 05 in the stack

- If not open, he reverses the ball back to 03, who has the whole right side of the court cleared for him to take the ball to the basket

- If O3 is denied the reversal, he will run a backdoor cut

O2

- Stacks with O3 and cuts off the double set by O4 and O5 to the corner, looking for a three

O3
- Waits for O2 to clear the double screen and then pops out hard to get a reversal pass from O1

- If he is overplayed, he back cuts hard to the basket

- If he catches the ball, he has a cleared side of the floor to go one-on-one

O4
- Starts on the top of a stack with O5, and, as O2 clears the double screen, O4 screens down on X5 so O5 can pop the stack

O5
- Starts on the bottom of the stack with O4 and sets a screen for O2 to get open in the corner

- Pops the stack and flashes into the near-side elbow

STACK SET—PLAY #3

This play is a counter for the previous play.

Diagram 116   **Diagram 117**

O1
- Dribbles the ball to the left wing

- Passes to 02 coming off the stacked double screen set by 04 and 05

- Can also keep the ball and feed 03 himself

02
- Catches the ball in the corner and waits for 03 to come to the block off a double screen

03
- Allows 02 to clear the double and starts to cut up as he did on the previous play

- After setting up his defender, he cuts hard back off a double screen set by 04 and 05 and goes to the ball-side block for the ball from either 01 or 02

04
- Screens for 02 going to the corner and then sets a double with 05 for 03 to post up

05
- Starts on the bottom of the stack with 04

- Screens for 02 going to the corner

- Next, he goes across the key with 04 to set a double for 03 to get open at the low post

STACK SET (DOUBLE LOW)—PLAY #4

Diagram 118

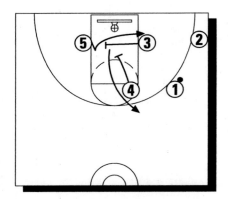

Diagram 119

01
- This set places all the decision making for the shot in 01's hands

- Dribbles the ball to the wing and reads O2 circling off the near-side stack to the corner and O3 in the post briefly

- Reads O5 coming to the ball-side post off O3's cross screen

- Third read is O3 coming off the down screen of O4 (screen the screener action)

O2
- Starts on the top of the stack with O3 and circles out to the corner and sets himself for either a three or a post feed

O3
- Lets O2 circle around him to the corner, then quickly turns and posts up briefly

- Crosses the key and screens for O5

- Receives the down screen from O4 and pops to the top of the circle, looking for a three

O4
- Starts on the bottom of the far-side stack with O5

- As the ball is dribbled to the wing, he pops to the elbow; and then, as O3 cross screens for O5, he screens down for O3

O5
- Waits for O3 to set the cross screen so he can go to the ball-side post

- Seals the defender and calls for the ball from either O1, O2 in the corner or O3 from the top

STACK SET (SINGLE)—PLAY #5

Diagram 120

Diagram 121

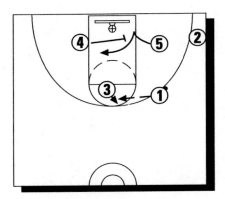

Diagram 122

O1

- Enters the ball to the wing with the dribble

- Reads O2 coming off the back screen, cutting to the basket before clearing to the corner

- Reverses the ball to O3 stepping off the back pick

- Screens down for O2

O2

- Cuts off the back screen set by O3, looking for the pass before going through to the ball-side corner

- Sets his man up and comes off O1's down screen after the reversal pass to O3

O3

- Pops out of the bottom of the stack with O5 and sets a back screen for O2

- Steps off the back screen and catches the reversal pass from O1

- Looks first for O5 coming off O4's cross screen, second for O4 rolling off the screen

- Third look is to O2 coming off the down screen

O4

- Starts on the opposite low block by himself

- Waits for the ball to be reversed and then sets a cross screen for O5

05

- Steps out to the perimeter as 01 dribbles the ball to the wing

- As 02 clears to the corner, he goes back in to the low block, posts and waits for the ball to be reversed

- As the ball is reversed to 03 at the top, he receives a cross screen from 04 and cuts over the top, looking for the ball

STACK SET (STAGGERED)—PLAY #6

Diagram 123

01

- Dribbles the ball to the left wing toward the low stack

- Reads 03 coming off the back screen set by 02

- Reads 03 again coming off the stack to the corner

- Reverses the ball to 02 stepping out from the back screen and screens down for 03

02

- As the ball is dribbled to the wing opposite, he sets a back screen for 03

- Steps back to the ball and catches the reversal pass from 01

- Reads 05 popping the stack and 03 coming off the down screen

03

- Starts on the top of the high stack with 02; as the ball is dribbled away from him, he steps out and then receives a back screen from 02

- Looks for the pass and then curls under the low stack to the corner

- As the ball is reversed, he receives a down screen from O1 and comes up looking for a shot

04
- Starts on the top of the low stack with O5

- After O3 has cleared the screen and the ball is reversed, he screens down on X5

05
- Starts on the bottom of the low stack with O4

- As the ball is reversed, O4 screens down on his man and O5 pops the stack into the key, looking for the high-low pass from O2

CHAPTER 4

Working from Other Sets

SINGLE LOW POST SET

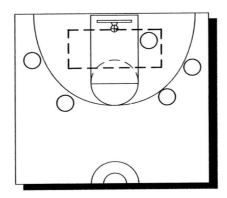

Diagram 124

The single low post set is usually used when a team has one player who is difficult to guard in the low post area. The other four positions can be perimeter players or can be interchangeable in the low post. The entire low post area is left vacant so that the one player can have all the space he needs to operate. If the four remaining players are good perimeter shooters, the defenders will not be able to collapse and help on the single post. If your single post is a great offensive rebounder, then this set will always keep him in a position to be around the basket.

It is essential that the perimeter players have the necessary passing skills so they can get the ball in to the post man. If the defensive team is dropping players off the perimeter players to help, the post man needs to be able to kick the ball back out. Splitting or screening off the post also adds a different dimension for the defense. In addition, proper balance and spacing also open up driving lanes for the perimeter players.

A team that has a smaller, quicker player who has the ability to score from the low post can create all kinds of problems for a defensive team. Their larger players can be taken away from the basket and will have more trouble trying to cover down on the post than smaller players. A coach can isolate a defender who is not used to playing by himself in the low post.

DOUBLE-POST SET—LOW OR HIGH-LOW

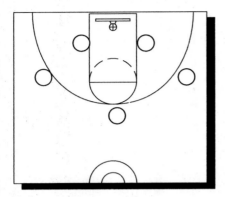

Diagram 125

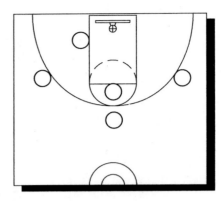

Diagram 126

If the personnel on your team includes two good post players, this set will allow you to utilize their strengths either individually or as partners. The posts can be placed in a double-low setup (Diagram 125) or in a high-low alignment (Diagram 126).

Using the two posts in a low set should be done when they are both large and maybe slower. This system can be adapted to produce close-in shooting, as well as screening possibilities and strong offensive rebounding position.

The perimeter players need to be able to feed the ball into the low post from the top and the wings, as well as shoot the ball when it is kicked out of the post. Opportunities for single and double screens exist both on the ball and off the ball for the perimeter players and on cross screens for post players.

Setting your post players in a high-low set gives your post players a little more operating room to get open. If one of the post players can pass, penetrate and shoot from the perimeter, then this set will be effective. If the two posts are interchangeable, they can require many defensive adjustments. This set also is one that can be used against both man and zone defenses. The set provides an excellent way to create clear-outs, post rubs and post back screens.

TRIPLE-POST SET

The triple post (Diagrams 127 and 128) is often used by coaches who have three strong inside players. They don't have to be big to be effective in this set, but they do have to be difficult to guard in the high or low post area. Placing three men close to the basket presents good single, double, diagonal and staggered screen situations. Also, it is very easy to run screen-the-screener out of this set.

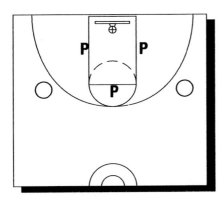

Diagram 127

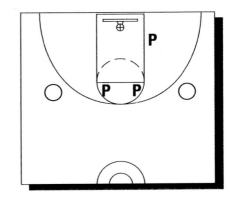

Diagram 128

This pattern does congest the key and allow the defense to help and recover a little better. The three posts need to be able to shoot from 15 feet, go hard to the offensive boards, screen for each other and pass the ball from post to post and from post to perimeter.

The two perimeter players must be good ball handlers, post feeders and shooters. They have to be able to get themselves open by using the posts as screeners.

OPEN-POST SET

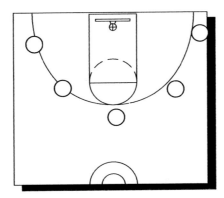

Diagram 129

An open post set (Diagram 129) will allow all five players a little more freedom of movement and provide them with many cutting and driving possibilities. All players are within one flash cut of receiving the ball in a position to be an immediate threat. The defense will have to decide if they are going to pressure or sag off, and both those strategies will open up plays for the offensive team.

If you have height, quickness or defensive mismatch advantages, they can be quickly exploited in this set. Double, single and staggered screens are easy to set up, as well as give-and-go, backdoor, flash and change-of-direction cuts. Cutters must quickly exit back to the perimeter to keep the center open for the next cutter or driver.

Although this setup does not lend itself to good offensive rebounding position, it does pull the defensive team away from the basket, often creating an advantage for the quicker team to get to a missed shot.

CONCLUSION

Set plays allow a coach to design an offense around the strengths and abilities of his players. Each year, your players will provide a different challenge for your coaching staff in selecting plays and sets that will give your present athletes the best chance of being successful. Three factors must be considered when choosing an offensive system:

1. It must be fundamentally sound.

2. It must fit the abilities of your players.

3. The coaches must understand the system thoroughly and be able to break it into drills and teach it effectively.

These three factors are all dependent on each other for team success. Your planning and confidence will be imparted to your players, and this will be essential for the offense to reach its maximum potential.

If the system you have chosen is not being productive, you may want to change it. But before you change, you should closely examine how the offense is being taught and practiced. No offense will work if the basics are not taught correctly and the fundamentals of screening and cutting are not being properly executed. More often than not, a sudden change results in the same problems the team had with the previous offense.

If you are thinking about making a change, devote time and study to the new system before installing it. Instead of starting an entirely new offense, perhaps you should think about making small variations in your existing offense. Before dropping the whole offense altogether, try to place your players in different positions or in a slightly different alignment. Remember that you are never too smart to learn from your opponents, your players or your colleagues.

I hope these plays will give you a basis for building an offense that works for your team. Remember, a few plays well executed will be more successful than many plays taught poorly and run without discipline.

Bob Huggins is a proven success as a program-builder, recruiter, game strategist and motivator. He has demonstrated this in a myriad of ways since joining the University of Cincinnati in 1989.

Inheriting a team that was short on numbers, Huggins inspired his initial team to a post season tournament and has done so every year since. Coach Huggins has compiled an impressive 247-82 record in his first 10 years at Cincinnati, making him the winningest coach in U. C. history.

For his efforts, Coach Huggins has been awarded many coaching honors, including the Ray Meyer Award as the Conference USA Coach of the Year in 1997 and 1998. He was also Basketball Times' selection for national coach of the year in 1997–'98, and was Playboy magazine's national coach of the year in 1992-'93.

Huggins began his coaching career as a graduate assistant at his alma mater, The University of West Virginia, in 1997. Subsequent coaching stints have included Ohio State (1978–'80), Walsh College (1980–'83), Central Florida (1983), and the University of Akron (1984–'89).

Born in Morgantown, W. Va., Huggins grew up in Gnadenhutten, Ohio where he played high school basketball for his father, Charles Huggins, at Gnadenhutten Indian Valley South. Bob and his wife, June, have two daughters, Jenna and Jacqueline.